SHADOWS

POETRY, TRIBUTES AND REFLECTIONS

Shadows are fleeting —

Look to the light ⁛

Dianne ⁛

SHADOWS

POETRY, TRIBUTES AND REFLECTIONS

By

Dianne Adair

𝔖𝔥𝔦𝔡𝔞𝔞𝔫𝔦𝔨𝔢𝔦

TORONTO

SHIDAANIKEI PUBLISHERS INCORPORATED – INCORPORATED IN CANADA
WWW.SHIDAANIKEI.COM
COVER DESIGN BY Dileen Simms, dileensimms.com.

LIBRARY AND ARCHIVES CANADA CATALOGUING IN PUBLICATION

Title: Shadows: poetry, tributes and reflections / Dianne Adair.
Names: Adair, Dianne, author.
Identifiers: Canadiana 2021009768X | ISBN 9781999225735 (softcover)
Classification: LCC PS8601.D33 S53 2021 | DDC C811/.6—dc23

PUBLISHED & PRINTED IN CANADA, 2021

Praises

With elegance and eloquence, Dianne has given poetic voice to the whispers of her own heart, the experiences of others, the groaning of society, and her generational legacy. In this book, you will find expressions of your own life in the words and in-between the lines. Woven in the variety of this masterpiece collection, are the much-needed avenues for healing, hope, empowerment, and ultimately, the overshadowing of our shadows.

Rev. Marva Tyndale
Director, Real Identity Discovery Ministries.

Shadows: Poetry, Tribute and Reflections is a "sensory adventure" that reveals the complexity of life as "an entanglement." The poet, Dianne Adair, emphasizes that "the shadows" can be engendered and enlightened through our "thoughts and actions." This anthology details not only Adair's personal perspectives on life and its various challenges, but the poet also seeks to give expression and meaning to others' experiences. Faith is an integral part of Dianne Adair and she espouses the importance of God, and His protection in the darkest moments. This is a constant theme in her poetry, especially in "*Let Me Find Him.*"

Adair's reflections whether the emotions and vulnerabilities evoked in "Fear," the invincibility of spirit portrayed in "Our Breath," the gutted honesty of "Scarred" and embodiments of strength as seen in her beloved "Una Mae," serve to remind us of the spectrum of emotions and life. As an essential dichotomy, Adair highlights where there are struggles, hope and endless possibilities as symbolized in "*Burning Flames*" and "*Unlock the Doors*." Genuine, revealing and inspiring are the words that epitomize the spirit of this book.

Dr. Lesley-Gail Atkinson Swaby
Founder and Managing Director,
Plum Valley Publishing Ltd., Jamaica.

Perhaps, it is Adair's tribute to Una Mae ("affectionately known as Cherry"), that captures the essence of this book. In the warm eulogy, Adair emphasizes the fullness of her departed friend's life, which included heartache and strife, deep enjoyment and laughter. Moving through an impossible diagnosis, Cherry still "left a legacy of faith and hope...," making her life a "pleasure to be a part of." Dianne Adair continues to find light in unlikely circumstances.

Amani Bin Shikhan
Freelance Culture Writer and Producer.

This Book is dedicated to the one who showed me life.
Mommy, I love you more than you know.

She worked hard all her life,
As a kid she crossed risky rivers
While balancing ground provisions on her head
So her sistas and brothas could be fed.

She grew up strong
And continued the struggle
When her kids came along,
A struggle to them, but a way of life for her
Doing anything to make ends meet
For her family to eat,
She cooked, fried fish and bammy,
Baked bun and other tasty delicacies sold
To the delight of many, her handiwork unfold.

Her hands were always in the fire
As she was also a hairdresser
Never did I see her crumble
She was always humble,
Grateful for life, her kids,
And the opportunity to give.

A disciplinarian she was too
Just one look and you knew
You betta behave or else...

She never made anything a bother
"I don't worry, I give it to the Father,"
She knew God never failed her yet
And I'm so grateful for the life she led
Cuz her example and love are forever felt

She will always be my beautiful,
Industrious and loving mother
Forever like no other.

"It's not how you start the journey that matters. But how you prepared, fought and visualized its end."
Dianne Adair.

Other books by the author

The Filament: Finding Fulfillment (2021).

Acknowledgements

To be able to express our pain and sorrows to family, friends and even strangers when in the valley of life can be such a relief. It brings healing to our being. We all have a story and sometimes, we have the same story that evokes myriads of emotions that can overwhelm us if not shared.

I am grateful for the bond I have with family and friends who impart encouraging words and support one another when the shadows block our light. The privilege to share these experiences in this book, to show the world that no one is alone, that they can heal through listening, speaking up and taking action, gives more than a glimmer of hope. It gives life and light to overshadow our shadows.

My wonderful family has always been a wealth of support with their patience and love. My husband Robert, son Maleik and especially my daughter Bobbi, who I constantly consult for her ideas and insight, have been so supportive. I am eternally indebted to you all. Words cannot adequately express my love.

Thanks to my mom Norma for her constant prayers, my dad Trevor and my sister Monique for their enduring love and encouragement. To my brothers and extended family, I am so blessed to have you in my life.

Where would we be without sisterhood? The bond between girlfriends tightens when the cords of life try to break us. The heavenly light shines even more when we pray, when we encourage one another, just call to say hello or go for a coffee.

Elsa, Wilda, Donna, Maxine, Pat, Dileen and Shellie, thank you for being some of my testers and warriors in prayer to see this book come to fruition. A special thanks to my dearest friend, Emily, who never stopped pushing me to finally publish this book of poetry and reflections. I appreciate and love you all.

To those who have given me permission to pay tribute to their departed loved ones, thank you for letting me keep their legacies alive in the pages of this book. My sincere thanks to all who have shared their inner most thoughts with me and the world. We are each other's story and victory.

Finally and most importantly, to the Most High God, I owe Him my life and my all. Without Him, I am nothing, and to Him I give all the glory and praise for this opportunity. He is my Lord and Savior, my light and my reason for living.

Reflections

A few years ago, I was on my bed lamenting, calling out to God for His divine help. As I quieted my spirit in his presence, He opened my eyes to the solution. I was sitting at the front of a wooden boat with my head looking up to the sky. On either side of me were tumultuous waves raging high. The surroundings were dark; the sky was black except for one beam of light coming from the heavens. I was at peace despite the storm.

 From my periphery, I noticed someone in the back of the boat quietly rowing while looking at me. As we journeyed through the storm together, I heard him speaking to my heart and in His still voice He said, "Be at peace, I will fight for you."

The shadows I face in this life will not be easy, but I'm safe because Christ is fighting for me and there is hope for a better tomorrow. Whatever challenges you face in the journey of life, we can share this vision of hope, light and love with the One who has overcome it all.

Sharing the experiences of life in this book of poetic reflections will hopefully leave you with not just hope and peace in the midst of the storm; but knowing that when we fight to breathe, to live as one race, as one of God's creations, it is worth it.

Preface

This collection is about any and everything felt and seen in life (whether literally, visionary or otherwise) through my eyes and the eyes of others. The intricacies of our lives encompass good and bad, success, challenges and disappointments. The chapter on **Life** captures some of these experiences; shadows of life. Knowing that God is always walking with us through every aspect of life's journey whether physical, spiritual, emotional or environmental is comforting knowing that He overshadows our shadows.

Tribute, honors those who have gained and shared their lived experiences through the ages and those who have gone on to another life, free from the 'cares' of this world. Their legacy lives on in so many ways – through God's grace in celebrating many birth years on this earth, to the lifetime bond in marriage and to the sweet memories of the love and life once shared before their last breath.

CONTENTS

Introduction

Life can be an entanglement. When we are trapped in life's shackles, we can either succumb to the pain of restraint, fear, or sorrow amidst the many challenges we face; or we can release our thoughts and actions to overcome our wounds and soar.

This collection of poems speaks to all of us, as we all have a story. It is not only told from an individual perspective, but also through the eyes of others as the author seeks to relay the messages and feelings that some cannot put into words. The emotion spills from the depths of the writer's heart and the heart of others, in an attempt to heal the pains we all have felt.

The intricacies of life should be expressed and celebrated. Release of any poison that eats away at us, and the ensuing relief, are necessary as we seek to heal and reduce our pain and sorrow. We should speak to each other and most of all to God, who will overshadow our shadows once we abide within Him.

There is always hope despite fear, love despite hate, success despite failure and joy despite sadness. Our lives may be shaded by a dim light at times, but that light can always get brighter and outshine the darkness, if we "take refuge in the shadow of God's wings"(Psalm 91:1).

"He that dwelleth in the secret place of the most high shall abide under the shadow of the Almighty."

Psalm 91:1 (KJV).

Life

"It's of no use being pregnant with great ideas unless their birth and timely growth bear fruits worth picking, worth re-producing." Dianne Adair

Life Line

My life is in you
Your breath saving me
Our blood lines stirred,
Preserved to prolong our lives
Yours in mine
Mine in yours.

Wonder

You wonder if anyone understands
The tingle through your veins
Your pain of a loved one
Killed in disdain and without restrain,
Just because you think his color is a stain
Not fitted for the fabric of your terrain.

You wonder does anyone take the time
To ponder the crisis that is ISIS?
When there are heard and unheard screams
Of inflicted agony as they massacre a colony,
Annihilating your spiritual and religious
Rights to serve Jesus Christ
A radical heist!

You wonder if the shame of your past
Will reappear,
Revealed to those you hold so dear
Things you never want them to hear.

You wonder if this world will ever get better
If the poor man living in the gutter
Will be treated kindly
Instead of being misled blindly
If the little girl or boy whose innocence
Is taken away will heal today
If the soldier's sacrifice,
Limbless
Mindless
Paid the price
You wonder.

But ponder no more
There's One who experienced
Your suffering
Who was willing to bear the buffering
Who promises a future
Of love and joy and peace
That will never cease,
So let your wonder ease.

More than a Quake

My heart bleeds
I have no sense of direction
Only confusion.

Where am I to start, my help to impart?
In a trance I walk-prying, grabbing debris buried
Hands big and small hold me tight
Then limp they go
Tears have no time to flow.

I dash to and fro to a faint voice here
A dangling foot there,
Some sign of hope I pray to save,
Thwarted by bodies pinned
With bare hands I pry
But hope is immediately dimmed
As another soul slips by.

Despair heightens as gasping
I speak to faceless hands and feet,
It's Mayhem in the streets as emotions fly high

As strewn bodies rise to the sky,
Higher and higher they pile!
Oh, how I want to wake
To be pinched from this dream
With its faint view of hope,
Help was needed decades ago.

"Today they see us, hear our cries,
Will they help before another one dies?
Maybe they will abandon us no more, oh may it be so!"

Burning Flames

Do you sometimes feel cornered, comatose?
Fighting the creeping cremation
Of your creativity that prevents
You from resurrecting
Or taking off as you hoped?

You constantly fan the fire,
Anticipating the burning flames
From wearily stoked sparks
To excitedly spread to your circle and beyond
To your mission of changing minds
To do well,
Of watering seeds to produce fruits.

As sticks gather around dry and ready ground,
Supportive voices of past
And present victories spur you on,
Helping to fan your flames
With hope anew,
Working hands and minds
Chant and prance to the music of

"Be brave and yes you can"
Igniting sleeping dreams
Awakening the corners
Of the mind to action.

It's time for unwavering smiles
The revelation of deep joy amidst the odds
It's time to spread the flames
To keep the legacy of our minds,
Our talents and our hopes alive!

Searching

In the silence of his mind
His thoughts screamed
From the heart.

A poignant pause in his life
His purpose unknown
Not wanting to live
Without a vision, a goal,
He searches.

His naked feet wandering
To paths on mother earth's soft ground,
Perhaps a trip to the continent,
To the motherland will open his eyes,
What a trip it was
Revelations of who he was and is
And to become.

Look around and see and feel
Take your time and connect and it will come,
No sooner and no later
Fire, passion, purity of heart

8

Will feed your purpose of life,
Of unity,
Action will come
It is coming
It is here
Be you in time!

Their Deaths in the Star Newspaper

She and hers perished
From that which she cherished
   A puff here and there
Not butting out with care.

With a flash her offspring
Went into the dark clouds of smoke
But Alas! A quick retreat, as he started to choke,
Could this 'fate' have been prevented
If she chose not to light one up?

Now the end of her vice
Has seen her demise and that of her spouse
How sad that their lives
Are now only rolled up
Into the thin pages of the news
With her son the star of her eye
Left behind to relive this sight.

Time Will Tell

With a whiff of hope
The scents of deliverance
Tease my mind and lighten my heart,
My distant view,
But still the darkness
Revolves, fighting to dismiss the light.

A puff of white lingers above
Unclouding my wavering thoughts and fears,
Hugs of support squeeze me tight
As Heaven's doors open wide,
I still hold on
Only time will tell.

Fear

Engulfed! Consumed! Enraged!
Boldness! Challenge! Tiredness!
Blackness! Tears
Some of the first words,
Images and mixed emotions
I exude as this word creeps up and attacks me!

Can I escape this suffocating blanket
Squeezing me tight
Straining my vocal cords day and night
From endless cries?

Why should I let a word
Entrap my thoughts?
Why ruin my time
And precious moments
With lifeless images
And feelings of just one word?
I must constantly crush and replace
Its ugly head until it is no more,
Substitute engaging, refreshing,

Livable words such as
Hope, change, happy, victory
Visceral responses
When facing my fears.

"Fear, I fear you no more.
You will come, but will surely go
I rise above as you succumb
To the freedom of a once enslaved mind!"

Our Breath

I will never fathom why
This beautiful dark skin
  Gives them pain and rage
Why they attack even my gaze
Why they play God to cut off my life
Always causing strife
Centuries of ropes, bullets, now hands and knees
No longer hiding behind a tree
They try to silence me
They don't care for the world to see.

I pity them
For their insecurity
Their lack of love and generosity
Their chokehold to stifle my creativity,
My ingenuity.

My emotions are high
And I will fight 'til I die
Not the same as they do
Cuz that's only a fool's adieu.

Cowards kill the body, not the mind, or soul
So we will fight until we are old
With intellect, mind and soul
And much more to unfold,
We are God's people,
This wilderness must end
For our people to live again.

Destiny

Who am I?
What am I really
Supposed to be?
Would the answer
Reveal my destiny?
God made me for a purpose
With different gifts,
Talents to make me
Focus on my destiny.

My life does not need to
End a certain way
I can divert its path,
Its destiny.

"I Rise, I Rise and I Rise"

I see my struggles
Fade, like an escape from a long charade
I look down the hills and valleys,
No longer brooding over my follies.
Standing tall on the mountain top
With a new song, a new dance
A new hop.

Down the line many things
Will be mine,
Dreams of success
Multiple things to bless
My days
My Nights
No more emotional fights.

To find success in failure,
Not failure in success,
Always sifting out and overcoming
My mess.

With my hands locked in the Father's above

"I Rise!"

Way beyond the skies,

"I Rise"

To the sweet sounds of victory,

"I Rise!"

Good Disappointment

As my ground rumbles,
Palms sweaty, heart over raced,
Face drops,
Shoulders plop
O' God, another disappointment
Now What?!
You promised this 'world' would be mine
Prosperity, Ingenuity and Creativity!

But my cobwebs are clouding
My paths to a better world,
Always getting my life hurled
In a direction that's twisted and curled
It only saps my soul, my joy and makes me sad.

"Why me?" I cry,
As sleep creeps in my darkness by and by
Then in the morning when
I rise,
I thank God I'm still Alive!
Given another day to hope, to pray
That God will help me find a way

To see the good in this trial,
If only He would turn my bitter to sweet,
Sweet Jesus, I need not always weep.

Then next week comes
And I receive some news
Allowing me to piece together
Things that made me confuse.

The light came on,
My eyes popped wide
My vision no longer to hide,
If the Lord had given me my desire,
Believe me it would leave me in the mire
It would leave a permanent scar on my tomorrows
All because of wallowing in my sorrows,
Neglecting to use my spiritual vision
To see Him sparing me from a terrible mission.

Chances

Roll the dice
What did you get?
That's how you live your life
On a bet?
"I bet you I can survive," you say
"If only I get that number I play."

Day in, day out, you try and try
Sometimes lucky enough to just get by
But is this how you really want to be
Without any feelings of security?
A chance here and a chance there
Never sure, always a dare.

When will this game end?
When will you turn the bend?
A passing bliss you can afford to miss
And find a life that's without the dice.

For the rest of us players,
A purposeful life will
More than suffice,

So let go of the cards,
The ticket and the dice
And flip this coin over
To start a new life.

Practicality

Encouragement is good and all
But how can this help me to stand tall
To get the right job, pay the bills, eat,
All the things I need to keep?

Well, it does provide some hope
And gives me the will to cope
I guess it ignites my faith
Shows me how I can create
Gives me ways to help shake up myself
Brushes off old ways
And actively seeks out better days.

To not just expect a miracle,
But work for one,
Putting my faith, hope and gifts into gear,
Into motion.

To first pray and seek
To go about it the right way,
So that there will be no delay
On the street to a practical day.

Not just the day,
But the nights and evenings too,
Showcasing the real you, the real me
Ending up in 'true practicality.'

Unlock the Doors

There are too many of them,
These locked doors!
From health to wealth,
Wisdom and understanding
From finance to romance,
So much more to escape
Please, unlock the doors!
Of freedom, joy,
Unexplained bliss,
The loosening of tightened fist.

Jaws gradually opening
The skipping of a joyful heart
Fears and doubt torn apart
To make way for a new start.

Sweet and fresh is the
Indescribable smell of hope,
Happiness and new beginnings,
The taste of tomorrow's endless winnings.

Spaces of possibilities,
Chainless hands and feet,
It's a pleasure to greet
No more the feel of clenched muscles,
The sound of emptiness
The sight of closed doors
In the way,
No more regrets or why.

Lessons learned of which path to take
Which door handles to shake,
New grounds have been broken
And endless possibilities
Awoken through unlocked doors!

Second Eye

You stare at me not looking at my face,
Expression or hearing my words,
Just piercing my very soul
Trying to understand the thoughts,
The meaning behind
The movements of my vocal cords,
Tearing away at the
Veneer of my words to find
The truth, me.

Wells of saltiness spring
Up masking my view
As you undress me
With your second eye.

Sadness, fear, desires, hopes and dreams
You undisguised in the crease of my eyes
My furrowed brows.

Your focus cuts through the façade,
Removing the tainted mask
To reveal the real me.

A sigh, slowly, steadily,
Unitedly escaped our lips,
Our eyes becoming one
All because of your second eye.

'Superman'

I am not as you think
Able to fill all your requests in a wink
Sometimes I need someone else to take care of me
Get inside my head, my heart and see
How they can for once cater for me.

I don't always express my worries out loud,
What clouds hang over my head or shroud
My heavy cloak sometimes pokes
With life's bits and pieces
That could easily choke,
Quickly soak my strength.

So maybe, just maybe, you can see my side
How sometimes I wish to hide
From the hustle and bustle of you...of my life.

To cut this cloak off with a knife
For a chance to soar
Above the azure skies
Without any shackling ties
For just a brief fling with my own life.

Survival

Sometimes you can go through
Rough waters whether self-inflicted or not
For weeks, months and years
That cause you to feel numb
To fighting its roughness,
To just even breathe;
Even periodic gasps of breath
To hold your head above the pull of defeat.

During the struggle, the flashes of your family,
Their disappointment, the sight of fear
For both of you never cease
To keep your arms flailing,
Your feet kicking to reach shore.

No, not even a thought of me at that moment,
Just being back on solid ground again
With us living as before
Happy, content, sure.

Beyond Failure

I welcome weakness,
Because of it I am strong
I can share my story
To all who come along.

Not viewing my follies as failure
But using them to work for the creator
Encouraging another
Providing support
Never a bother
To show how you can
End up with a good report.

My faults bring forth hidden
Treasures within love, hope, joy,
Dependency on Him,
Seeking,
Searching to know how to overcome
With God's help it will be done.

I hear the sweet sounds of Hallelujah
Songs in my head,
As my victories spread
To those I love so dear
And others both far and near.

No more faltering before me?
Of course not!
But I will ride over each one surely,
Up and over I go
Yesterday, today, tomorrow
My journey flows
Into lands of mines ready to blow
To reveal a new show
Of a life ready to live beyond my failure.

Some People, Part 1

Such rude obnoxious creatures
Displaying aloof, venomous features
The sting of their icy demeanor
Leaves a draining emotional mark...
A stain that one must quickly remove
Before it filters one's every groove
Becoming infected by their mood.

You must disinfect their 'offensive smell'
Before it poisons, breaks through your shell
Making you unwell.

What's their problem?
Do they feel their attitude can solve them?
As they attack and shatter
With twisted words and faces bent
Insulting, catapulting
To one so undeserving.

Abrasive, ignorant, color-sighted and sour
Always extending your so-called power,
Sneering at others not like you
Not caring who you offend
Many or a few.

Your lack of respect is truly
A reflection of your innermost *depth*
As deep as the ocean
Your words do sink beneath my skin,
With a grimace I wince,
Your venomous features
Gleam bright in red light
As I swallow back your bile
And seek my heavenly light.

Some People, Part II

Maybe some people
Are unkind and mean
But perhaps that's only how it seems
Perhaps they are hurting inside
And just wish to hide
By adorning a mask
That is not reflective of them
Hoping that someone will peep within
Revealing who they really are
Starving for forgiveness, friendship,
Hope to be near not far.

Perhaps they are longed to be loved
Instead of always being shoved...
Perhaps they were rejected by many
And therefore know not how
To give anything good in return.

Underneath the thick skin of visible hate
Is a soul crying out for someone to take
Their bitterness and turn it aside,

Into sweetness
They will have no need to hide
Perhaps their attitude is a mirror of you.

Known

In the mirror I stare
A beautiful face I see
Chiseled with time's lines
Perfectly imperfect, Known and unknown
A work in progress.

These secret eyes reflect inner thoughts
Years lived and this moment in time
Eyes wide opened for the world to see.

Who do I see?
My truth is important to me
A myriad of things stares back at me
Past time and present flashes on my screen,
Pain, sorrow, fear, sacrifice and bliss
Love, hope, happiness, black and whiteness...
Things to overcome and the race to run
But the ultimate me is God's masterpiece
One day to be fully known.

Being Me

The D is for Dianne
Decidedly Dianne
I *gotta* be me
It's who God wants me to be
A woman that is patterned after Him
His love and grace seen from within.

I *gotta* be me
Crazy and free
With my curly sometimes natty head
And my ways sometimes misread
To sing even if I can't
To dance and prance
To give love, sympathize
Hugging as I empathize
I just *gotta* be me
Always encouraging others to be
Hopeful and trust in God
Even when flooded with the bad.

Sometimes I'm passive-aggressive
And although that may have its place
I often have to ask for extra grace
To curtail my wayward ways
I dream, aim for better
To cast off my fetter
For God's satisfaction,
I *gotta* be me
I *gotta* be who He wants me to be.

A Moment of Weakness

Have you ever had one?
A moment of weakness?
As the words flew out of your mouth,
You knew instantly it was a mistake!
Whether vulnerable by your own error
Or life's inevitable circumstances,
You knew it shouldn't have happened,
Ever thought or said.

Your misty mind, jumbled thoughts
And unclear brain waves
Triggered a thoughtless signal,
And now its jolt of reality is too late.

Was it a moment
You could have controlled?
Words that immediately felt
A bitter blow churning
Your stomach with regret?
"I'm sorry, don't hold it against me,
It was a moment of weakness."

Then your gentle forgiving words
Soothed my foolish utterance,
Erasing it as if never known
Thank you.

Moving On

You constantly chew up yourself
For presumably a 'never should be bond'
Too critical of what you both say and do.

Tired of treading in the past
Constantly swirling in 'What ifs'
And in and out of
'I should or shouldn't' shifts.

I need to trap this remorse of time,
Its infiltration of today
And blurriness of the dawn
Should I? Do I work to the bone
On forgetting and forgiving?
I do try, not as much as I should.

Resentment and misery should go
Sweet nothings and gratefulness
Instead should flow
Not being this fidgety
About every 'nitty gritty.'

Staring less blindly into the glass of peace
Seeing compromise, acceptance
And happiness within reach
Hoping the turmoil will cease.

Then suddenly the glass shatters,
Revealing what really matters...

Choices

The cost weighs heavily,
Afflicting pain or giving joy
As they segue to offspring present and future
Choices, their consequences
Weave into innocent lives
Choices, they begin and end with me.

Afterthought

I was impulsive in saying no, I
didn't want it to be so,
I let self in the way,
Even though I had so much
To say,
Regrets always come after,
Not much can be done with the matter.

Always capture the moment,
As it will be forever taken...
To encourage, admonish or praise,
To tell the story of life,
That will profoundly affect our days.

You Don't Love Me

Love you say is nothing else
But giving,
Sacrificing your time and feelings
Everything wholeheartedly,
Making the time to do for me,
Know me, and cater for me.

You say:
"There's no true or perfect love,
Just love"
"For what is love if a description precedes it?
Does it need to be reciprocated if it's love?"

Love is more than caring,
Respect or giving
Not because of having too much
Or making a show to those
You do or do not know
But wisely imparting all of you
A choice the mind is free to make.

You say you don't see my love,
Hear my love, feel my love
"You don't love me anymore"
How do you really know?

Let Me Find Him

What's wrong
 Why are you crying my child
Don't say you don't know,
Someone troubled you?
Something?
There must be a reason
You're too young for these hidden feelings.

Don't let them consume you
I want to know,
Share it with me
Come my child, don't cry,
Let's talk, it will work out fine.

In the silent turmoil of my head,
Drained with ideas of what to do,
I suddenly felt a trickle on my face,
Then a steady flow
Drenching my soul as I hold him close,
Squeeze him tight.

"Show me what to do, God,
What to say,
How to make it right."
Tomorrow has to be bright.

This will not dampen our hope for a better day
"Come child, let's talk, read, write,
Say and do all we can to get through,
It will be alright!
It's just time."

"See! Look at your tomorrow,
Your smile brightly shining
Like the star you truly are
It's going to be fine my child,"
It already is...

Better Than Before

OH NO! MY GOD!
Hands over mouth,
Eyes popped wide,
Motionless you stand as her body
Crashed to the ground.

A BIG BANG! Crackling sounds
Is that a bone? **Dear God NO!**
NOT HER NECK
I'M SCARED TO CHECK!
With drained blood, heavy feet
And trembling hands
To her side you go
With hopes that
Your fears are not so.

Then reality hits like
A vengeful storm
Cutting off the lights of her youth,
Her promise.

No more running, walking,
Jumping or prancing?
With shoulders squared
With a sweeping tower of strength,
I prepare to challenge this scare
I won't succumb to its fear!
No more negative reflections,
Only future projections
Of hope, a restored young body,
A happy soul.

"It's just for a time my dear,
A momentary pause,
Then off you go steadily rising,
Smiling, running,
Jumping better than before..."

Hurdle

Hurdle over hurdle we go
In life's fear we bask
We glow
With sublime feat,
We strive for the finish line.

Instead of

Instead of flames
Smoke
Instead of death
Hope
Instead of cries of blame
Silence
Instead of tragedy
Redemption
Instead of devastation
Joy.

Piercing through
The dissipating smoke
I see you watching me
See you saving me,
Teaching, reminding me...
About five hours of intense flame
Saturated in one spot,
A foray with the burning pot
Just in time you made it stop
 "O God!" was all I could say,
As we did everything

To get the smoke away
We thought of what could have been
Screaming sirens, blame,
Shame, horrific images
Of no more
But because of God's grace
Instead of echoed no more.

Holding My Breath

Breathe, breathe, breathe
I wish I could breathe
Bottled up inside
I struggle to exhale
To release pains, regrets, disobedience
And fears that cost me happiness and peace.

Sometimes I sniff the sweet scent
Of freedom and joy
Slowly, steadily I exhale,
Hoping to fully deflate
Only to hold my breath again.

With swirling thoughts in my head,
My eyes visualize the feeling of hope,
And I learn to laugh and breathe again,
Until another storm hits
And I hold my breath again.

Ice Storm

Pellets of ice dripping in droves
Masking everything as it grows
A heavenly beauty,
A glistening spectacle.

Despite damages to power lines
And homes plunged into darkened mines
Nothing could erase the beauty of the ice.

Snap! Snap! Snap! Cameras flashing
Before crack! crack! crack!
The ice goes crashing.

Constantly in awe, we look around
As ice junks spread on the ground
This spectacular sight was
A captivating sheet of white.

Wasted Opportunity

Every day
It's a new breath
And opportunities come anew.

Many are screaming out for
A chance to speak
But are silenced by
Fear of retribution and death,
Where does your breath flow?
Does it elevate, does it disintegrate
Or does it praise?

Have a purposeful breath
Prioritize your breath to worship,
To love, to honor and praise.

Whisper sweet words to lovers
Be uplifting to all you come across
Opportunity may only come by once,
We hope to never have to regret
Because of wasted opportunities.

'Normal'

Screams! Fire!
Flying foes melting human flesh!
Crashes, ashes, machines spraying
Aimlessly at the innocent.

This is the New Norm!
Power hungry prowlers and strikers,
Overthrowing, dehumanizing,
Enslaving and kidnapping for selfish gain,
All in the name of religion!
With no regard for life these revelers,
Self-pleasers, and pleasure
Seekers have a field day.

They wipe out smiling faces
Of young and old, families and cities
No peace anymore, it's Mayhem!
The New Norm!

'Poised'

Facial beauty,
  Perfect body tone
Flawless skin, rich and taut
Attractive Attire
Forever consumed appearances
Always on fire!

Hair in the latest fashion
Dangling jewels adorn
Stance competing with the giraffe
High above all
You pose
Poised.

Flashing lights
Endless selfies
"I'm it! Look at me, my car,
My stuff, my success"
Yet you fail to see the effect
That in a jiffy beauty melts

When the creator takes you back
When you look behind the façade
You realize you are the same as them all
An empty face chilled and poised.

No flashing lights
No one to admire
Just a shell with a soul stilled,
Poised?

Crippled

What images flash through your mind?
A man or woman's fractured body
Holding a cane or in a chair confined?
Possibly our world today
The crisis, ISIS?

Do you imagine recruitment
Of young flesh painting the world red?
Perhaps a life filled with dread?
Or having a voice without words
Or having words without a sound?

Do these images or flashes blind
You with no hope of tomorrow?
Or do you see an end to this sorrow?
Do you see a mind cringing with lived experiences
Of abuse with shocking images
Of overt or covert trauma?
Or invisible scars, reflective
In stupor or silence
Or screams of inexpressible pain?
Or do you see a carbon copy

Of yourself, a human being
Wrangled by life's woes
In need of affection
From your head to your crippled toes?

Do you have the hope
Of a stricken life being healed
By a stretched out hand
Straightening your feet to walk,
To climb higher and higher?
Is there someone in front
Or behind nudging
You towards possibilities,
Enhancing your capabilities?

Kite in the Sky

A sunny day in the park,
Will it last?
She runs in the wind,
Her kite flying high
Her parents watching
Close by.

The bliss of this sweet
By and by
No danger lurking?
She knew somehow
That ain't working
Her skin told her so

And when she grows
The memories of that
Day keep resurfacing
Hoping for her kite
To always fly in the sky.

Now

I choose now!
Now to speak
Now to sing
Now to dance
Now to live
Now to love

I choose now to dream
Now to pray
Now to choose
Because now is guaranteed,
Not yesterday, today or tomorrow
I Choose Now!

Scarred

This poem ("Scarred") reflects the experiences of a dear friend, who through hurt and pain has embraced forgiveness. She is strengthened and her faith in God is renewed.

I gave you my all
My heart
A big part of me!

My mind shared delicacies
Of inner matter,
Of sacred thoughts unfold
You opened my door
With your words of love
Only for me, only for me
It felt so surreal, this bliss I felt.

My fragility fought off fears
And doubts with your assurance,
And love grew fast into weeks and months
Love etched forever in my beating heart

Dancing to the rhythm of
An endless flow from
Your sweetness and care.

Then one unforeseen day
The collapse came
The crush of forever...
Promises immobilized
Marred
Scarred my bleeding heart.

Months and years passed
With the pain of lies and disrespect
Empty promise,
Burning pangs of your
Infidelity shifted my heart
Staving off others to taste of my love.

It's been too long
I pray God forgive my thoughts
Of a pound of flesh

To forget the lingering freshness
Of this stain and rise again to heal
To love again
And so it will be as only time wins.

Forward, March!

We have been marching for decades
Thousands made up the brigade
Ready, Set, Go!
Many times we did so,
But how much have we progressed?

A step here and a step there
And then we regress
But we will keep hope alive as all is not lost
Step back and set backs will come
As we learn and re-deploy until we've won
And winning is not what we just want
But for all to learn we are all apart
Of one race, one blood, one family
Being human is not an anomaly.

No matter how we look
We should all embrace,
Our diversity is not a disgrace
But God meant it as a beautiful thing
To celebrate

Not to curse, kill or hate

No man is an island,

We need each other

So let's love and work

Together because that is real power.

Tribute

"The beginning and end of many things depend on you."
Dianne Adair

Norma

She's everyone's cheer
Always a bright smile
A gentle touch,
A 'how are you' or 'hello dear.'

She's a pleasure to meet
To greet,
Bringing an unending bond of friendship,
A genuine care to those far and near
A simply beautiful person inside and out!

Always upbeat
Sharing with those in need of her time,
Listening, always encouraging.

Someone who will laugh with you
Listen to your fears, share your tears,
Your joys, your tomorrows.

A mom who loves life, music,
Is fun to be around,
Her advice is always sound.

She takes risks,
Loves the camera
Her pictures captivate her pleasant,
Blissful aura.

Norma has a passion for beauty,
A love for flowers
Of baking, dancing, singing
And did we say picture taking?

A prayer warrior is she for her children
And strangers too,
A confidante to me and to you.

She's a light on your dark days
And always knows how to calm your ways
A true role model
Incomparable to no other,
Deeply loved
She's our mother!

Fifty (50) Years of Love

This is a story more than
Fifty years in the making,
A story of love's first bite
A story of two people creating,
A life long journey of golden light.

Like the timely
Arduous work it takes to refine gold,
And the joy
Sweat and tears in changes untold,
So is the life of mom and dad,
More than fifty years old.

From the tender age of thirteen
She looked down from the balcony above,
And there was her Prince Charming,
Looking up at the beauty of his Dove.

With butterflies buzzing
Within both him and her,
So the story began
With just a simple stir.

From adolescence to adulthood,
To golden years,
They lived, loved, laughed
And even shed some tears.

Many fears they faced in their life
From a burnt down home
To the scars of a surgeon's knife.

But through it all
They gained more than they lost,
Because their love and friendship
Survived at all cost.

Both are beautiful, inside and out
Kind and compassionate
On them you can always count.

I thank God for both of you
And your love so dear,
And for a legacy of light
For us to adhere.

Thank you mommy and daddy
For who you are
And for a memorable journey
Of over fifty years thus far.

Mother D

GRANDMA
GREAT GRAND
GREAT, GREAT GRAND

February 2015

She was a picture of strength, character and beauty intricately woven to form you and me, descendants of a remarkable woman. She was a fighter. In her life she fought against the odds of hardship while nurturing her children and others' children.

A gift to each life she touched where shades of integrity, kindness and love were left behind her. A transference of her inner beauty shone beyond the doors of her home and offspring and traces of her light can be found in various communities and even countries.

Mother D was a trailblazer in character and quality. She encompassed a spirit of humanitarianism, always ready and willing to help others in need. She had a quiet disposition, but possessed an empowered personality and admirable work ethics.

Echoes of Mother D can be heard in her legacy, her children, her children's children and in all who were privileged to know her. Her virtue of a sweet and gentle spirit, of kindness, patience and a heart of love lingers on; a persona worthy to be passed on.

I admired her strength throughout the years, her love of her 'roots' never ceased to amaze and enlighten me; from her firmly grounded family tree, to her hobby of gathering the varied species of plants, bushes and flowers she deemed useful. She had a 'raw' aptitude for naturopathic medicine, regularly engaging in healing practices with these 'roots,' her different concoctions and spirited solutions.

I will always remember when I was a little girl and would sleep walk from time to time. She took me one day (with her head skillfully wrapped and in her traditional white clothing) and spun me around and around, trying to get rid of this 'evil spirit,' that caused me to sleep walk. Her foundation of pride yet humility stood tall in the face of fear, fighting with diligence for the survival of herself and her family.

"Mother D, I will miss your quiet laughter, your soul searching stare, your healing bushes and your love of walking for miles and miles on end. Although your mind wandered and saw places we could not see, although your body faltered and felt pains we could neither feel nor your roots could heal, your lessons of love and kindness live on forever."

My mother, your mother, granny, she has given a legacy of endurance against all odds and life both intricate and beautiful; a human mosaic worthy of emulation.

Until the final chapter of each of our stories reunites us, rest sweetly in the arms of our Lord, Mother D.

Una Mae
Affectionately known as Cherry
March 2017

She once told me why people called her Cherry, but I had my own thoughts on the reason for her nickname. A cherry is a bright, usually sweet colorful fruit; an attractive topping on the finishing touches of an ice cream sundae or an iced cake. Its bright red color stands out and makes a bold statement and its taste is a partaker's delight.

That was my dear family friend, defender and adviser, Cherry. She had a big personality, a big heart and a sweet, caring spirit. Her confidence exuded the strength of a woman who knew the importance of taking charge and at the same time the common sense to know that her physical empowerment was only dependent on the grace of God. Her beloved family was her pride and joy; she beamed with pride when she spoke of their love and support.

Cherry loved to cook and she loved her food! Most of us have witnessed her culinary skills. It was always a delight for her to share her cooking with others. She loved life and celebrated it to the fullest, whether it was a birthday party or opening her home every New Year's Day to celebrate with family and friends.

It didn't matter how sick or tired she felt, she would cook up a storm and bake her delicious cakes and corn bread. In the evening after her hard work, she would sit at the table and her eyes would circulate the room. The satisfaction on her face was as palatable as the food. The joy in seeing everyone eating, chatting, laughing and just having a good old time was like the cherry on top and a perfect end to an event that she loved and had hoped to continue for a long time.

I often smile when I think about her dry sense of humor. I could understand when she said her favorite show was Coronation Street. She watched every episode. She wasn't afraid to make fun of herself; whether it was her appearance or something she did, often quoting some Jamaican saying to emphasize her point.

She was a realist. If you wanted an honest opinion, you just had to ask her; she would tell you like it is because she was genuine and wanted the same in return. Once you had her as a friend, she was a friend indeed- encouraging, always calling if she hasn't heard from you and sometimes even sending you messages on Whatsapp, once she got the hang of it.

Cherry had a strong and commanding disposition. She was a leader, an advocate for many - her family, friends and co-workers. Her advice was genuine and her admonishment when given was food for thought.

When she was diagnosed with cancer, she was told nothing could be done for her. The surgeons closed her up and that was it. But Cherry was a fighter and eventually gained the strength and courage to fight for her life. After accepting Christ as her Savior, her faith and hope heightened as she was determined to beat this disease. And so she did for many years with lots of prayer, encouragement and hard work.

She stood tall in the face of despair and failing health and fought with all her might, and with God's mercy to live 23 years after being diagnosed with cancer. Cherry may not have lived to see the 70 years she hoped for, but God knew that she needed to rest from years of pain and suffering. He took her home to be with Him. She "fought a good fight, she kept the faith and she finished the course."

She has touched us all in some way. She left a legacy of faith and hope for us to emulate despite life's challenges, a tradition of celebrating life and love and an example of true friendship. It was indeed a pleasure to be a part of her life. We will miss you, Una Mae - our sweet Cherry. Rest in Peace.

Ruth

February 2019

When I was told in 1991 that I would be getting a new Director of Nursing at our Long Term Care Home, I wondered who she was. This query must have been evident on my expression as I was told, "she is a very nice person and has been working at the home for years."

I suppose Joyce, one of the managers, wanted to appease any concerns I had knowing that as the nurse in charge, I would be reporting directly to her. Little did we know that this was the start of a professional and personal relationship with Mrs. English that lasted a life time.

On the day of our first meeting, I was immediately struck by her height, but more so by an elegance and kind demeanor that surpassed her physical stature. She had a pleasant and captivating aura and immediately I felt at ease.

During the years that we worked together, she was gentle but firm; a stickler who ensured and encouraged the staff to do the right thing. Mrs. English would often walk the corridors of the nursing home checking in on residents and staff to make certain all was well. Sometimes, she would come to work early in the morning and would try to tip toe ever so quietly so that we wouldn't hear her coming, but the sound of her heels always gave her away.

I think people are attracted to fairness, dedication and hard work and Mrs. English exemplified these and so much more. I was told that prior to her being appointed the Director of Nursing that she worked in another area of the Nursing Home, where she served patients their medication, even with a broken arm that was placed in a cast.

She refused to let the residents or staff go without the quality of care they needed and would fill the gap of the nursing shortage despite her broken arm. This didn't just indicate the dedication she had to her nursing profession, but her sheer selflessness, integrity and loyalty.

The exact time of our transition from being my boss to becoming my friend, spiritual mother, confidante, coffee mate and so much more is a bit vague. I guess we just segued into these roles after her retirement; that was when she insisted I call her Ruth.

Believe me it took more than a few tries to get it right! Even though she moved miles away after her retirement, we found time to meet, to call each other and to write. She even invited my kids and I to spend a weekend at her country home where we played card games, went for walks and later she treated us to homemade cookies and pies. To this day, my daughter still claims Ruth's homemade jam and apple crumble was the best she's ever had!

I always cherished our rendezvous at Tim Hortons after our yearly Long Term Care reunion. That was our go-to spot where we overindulged in sweet snacks and hot beverages. She would often say, "Dianne, I really shouldn't be having all these sweets," and I would say, "me too, Ruth."

We would laugh our heads off and before we knew it the delights were all gone. That's one of the things I liked about Ruth and that we had in common. We could both have a hearty laugh when we said or heard something funny. She would throw her head back, close her eyes and have a good old laugh.

Like two little kids ourselves, we chatted about our kids and a myriad of other things going on in our lives; but more than anything else, we talked about and prayed to our Lord and

Savior Jesus Christ. Ruth and I had quite a few things in common, but I think the longevity of our friendship was based on a spiritual foundation. We both loved our Lord and most of our time was spent with Him.

She was a private person and I was privileged to have shared in the life of such a phenomenal woman. When Ruth moved back to the city, we would regularly meet for lunch (usually at her condo) where I would be greeted with freshly baked cookies and enjoyed many sumptuous meals on a table spread with the finest china. We would catch up on the kids, on my new job, my mission's trips and her health.

We often read or talked about the devotional I gave her called "Jesus Calling" and the comfort and peace it offered. We made it a duty to pray together. She always put others first and was an exceptional listener. Ruth would listen as I would rant and rave about the intricacies of my work and life, then she would fill me in on hers.

Our plan for another rendezvous was to go to a different coffee place called Aroma that I wanted to try; but this wasn't meant to be. She became ill in 2018. When she shared her prognosis with me via email, that she had weeks to months, but definitely not a year, the shock and sting of the news had me in a daze for weeks as I grappled with the thought of losing my dear Ruth.

But in true 'Ruth style,' exemplifying love and care for her God and others, she ended her e-mail with, "Thank you so much still for your prayers, they mean so much and God is so good and always with me. Hope that all is well with you and your lovely family. Love, Ruth."

 She was forever grateful to God and to her children for their love and support. She wasn't able to write to me after that, but I was grateful for her daughter who kept me abreast of her condition.

Our last conversation on the phone was filled with tears and a sweet sorrow. She actually called to thank me for a letter and flowers I sent her and, again in true 'Ruth style,' asked me how the kids and my husband were doing. My kids and family had the highest respect and admiration for her. An elegant woman of quiet strength and a complete dependence on God was Ruth.

So Ruth, this is my last e-mail to you until I see you again. I miss you more than words can say, but I can just imagine as you tilt your head back, close your eyes and with a newfound laughter as you embrace your Lord and long gone loved ones, how happy you are now. What a blessing and a gift you were to us. In a way, I'm glad we didn't go to that new coffee shop because I would rather remember the sweet essence of our favorite meeting place, an aroma that lasted a life time for us. You are at peace now and once again thank you for your legacy and shining example of love, kindness, of grace, humility, prayer and most of all, your love and devotion to your Lord and Savior, Jesus Christ.

Sleep sweetly, Ruth English.

Love always,
Dianne.

Life Goes On...

I lived
I died
And then I live again,
This time for eternity
The best living yet,
Live well.